AUTHOR

Jenn Labin
Jenn Labin, chief talent and diversity officer at MentorcliQ, has more than 20 years of experience in talent development, training, and design. Previously, she was the owner of TERP Associates, which MentorcliQ recently acquired. Labin is a presenter and author of *Mentoring Programs That Work*, a unique approach to building scalable and sustainable mentoring programs.

Content Manager, My Career
Lisa Spinelli

Editor, *TD at Work*
Patty Gaul

Managing Editor
Joy Metcalf

Graphic Designer
Shirley E.M. Raybuck

Mentoring has developed during the past few decades to provide the exceptional benefits of a social learning relationship. Research continually demonstrates the impact of mentoring on everything from job performance to talent pool mobility to employee engagement and retention.

In fact, a study with Clorox shows—according to its figures—a 19-fold return on investment for its internal structured mentoring programs. Data that Cardinal Health collected on its own program reveals that participants with two or more mentoring relationships are twice as likely to stay with the organization.

Talent development practitioners have started gaining ground in introducing formal or structured mentoring programs internally to achieve great results in leadership development, career planning, diversity and inclusion, and more.

During my 20 years of professional experience, my mission has been to help support talent development practitioners who are leveraging mentorships internally. These practitioners have increasingly raised a flag in our interactions that, while they are committed to bringing mentoring to the talent they are responsible for, they have been unable to benefit from those types of relationships.

Sometimes talent development professionals themselves aren't sure where to turn for a positive and valuable mentoring experience. Occasionally, they may have tried to reach out to a potential mentor and the experience didn't work out well. For some, unfortunately, in rare circumstances, the mentors they found have done more harm than good. Still, mentorships are most often valuable, and all individuals—talent development professionals included—should seek out these opportunities.

In this issue of TD at Work, I will
- Demonstrate the value of finding a mentor for any stage of your career.
- Show the different types of mentoring relationships.
- Describe how to build significant mentoring relationship with trust and respect.
- Talk about the importance of setting expectations and developmental goals.
- Equip you with practical tools for achieving your learning goals.

Mentoring Benefits

Mentoring, coaching, and *sponsorship* are all words that the talent development or HR industry uses to describe social learning relationships. Those words are sometimes used interchangeably, and sometimes have specific and different meanings. For this issue of TD at Work, *mentoring* refers to a relationship built on mutual trust for the purpose of learning and growing as a professional.

Social learning relationships are consistently the most effective methods for developing talent, including yourself. According to Panopto, a learning software company, "Social and collaborative learning may be one of humankind's oldest forms of learning. At its essence, social learning is the continuous process of learning from other people. We are learning socially when we observe other people, ask questions, and share knowledge resources." Social learning through mentoring opens networks, improves skills, and empowers participants.

Not only is mentoring an important developmental tool, it's especially effective for increasing diversity and building an inclusive culture. According to a 2017 study by executive search firm Heidrick & Struggles that surveyed more than 1,000 professionals, mentoring relationships were most important to women, along with racial and ethnic minorities. Because of the relationships that

---

Hollywood's Single Mentor Myth

What do *Star Wars'* Yoda, *Back to the Future's* Doc Brown, *Harry Potter's* Albus Dumbledore, and *The Karate Kid's* Mr. Miyagi have in common? They are some of the greatest mentors to have graced the movie screen. Joseph Campbell's formula, from his renowned work *The Hero's Journey,* says that a mentor helps a hero transition from a state of general obliviousness to an awareness of the imbalance of the universe. The mentor then provides training and tools so that the hero can go forth and independently right the wrongs in the world—or take down Cobra Kai, as in *The Karate Kid.*

The problem with these fictional mentors is just that: They aren't real. Popular culture teaches us that if we are deserving, a magical influence will arrive and hand us the keys to a perfect future. This is an unrealistic idea and even harmful in many ways. It creates the expectation that a perfect mentor will arrive to address all our skills gaps without any effort on our part.

In reality, the best way to progress in various developmental areas is to find different mentors who each bring unique expertise. Be mindful as to how you use the relationships, though. Seek to build each mentoring partnership as appropriate for your career stage and path. For example, if you are early in your career, you likely won't seek to develop your executive presence. And if you don't plan to seek a managerial or leadership role, you may never opt for this goal.

Remember, everything doesn't have to happen at the same time. Spending quality time and effort on each step of the journey will help you build a foundation for later experiences and successes.

they had with their mentors, the respondents said they felt more supported, were exposed to more opportunities, had a clearer vision of their contributions to organizational goals, and had more effective relationships with co-workers across different teams.

That is not only great for employees but also for the organization. McKinsey studies indicate that inclusion—which the company defines as openness, equality, and belonging—can show positive results in recruitment and retention, organizational profitability, and creating value for customers and stakeholders. Mentoring is clearly a win-win for everyone involved.

In real life, mentors who have a lasting affect on your career start out working with you on specific development areas. The learning-focused relationship often develops over the years, leading to more robust, deeper, and broader discussions. However, the mentoring relationship must build a strong foundation of trust and learning.

Early in my career, I participated in a talent review meeting with the executive team of a large sales organization. Throughout the meeting, the leaders identified some of their team members as high potentials, well placed, or at risk. The executives had an easy time labeling individuals as high potentials when they had developed deeper relationships and taken these individuals on as informal mentees.

For the chosen few, that meant they would receive further investment—in the form of training, formal mentorship, and stretch opportunities. Meanwhile, everyone else was unlikely to see much investment at all. That was the first time I saw the power of mentoring at play.

The world runs on relationships and connections. Mentorship is just one form of relationship—and it's powerful. A stellar mentor can provide incredible opportunities, greatly expand your network, and change the trajectory of your career.

I have had the honor of working with many mentors over my career:

- Elaine has been the catalyst for many of my professional accomplishments. I hope to match her achievements in my chosen field.
- Charlie works in a different field and offers unique and innovative practices.
- Nancy's success is incredible, and her mentorship has been about authentic leadership.

Outside of professional areas of expertise, I even have several mentors for health and parenting. Given the benefits that can come from having an effective mentoring relationship, everyone should have at least one professional mentor during their career.

Know Your Purpose

Before you think about finding a mentor, you first need to know the purpose behind the desired relationship—know the why, what, when, and how before jumping into a mentoring relationship. Finding a mentor who will help guide you and will ask great questions depends on the information you are pursuing.

- Why are you seeking a mentor?
- What do you want the individual to help you with?
- When and how often will you meet?
- How will conversations take place?

Look for a mentor for an identified area of growth. No single person will serve all purposes. The more clarity you have about your mentoring journey, the better off you will be. The last thing you want to do is start on this journey with no discernable plan in place. A plan will help you narrow your search to potential mentors who will be a good fit in the specific areas that make sense for you.

While this may seem like common sense, it definitely isn't common practice. One of the most frequent mistakes I see practitioners make is deciding they want to be mentored but they can't explain the purpose for that desire. Mentors aren't typically excited to work with a mentee who approaches them with little clarity about their plans.

> **The more clarity you have about your mentoring journey, the better off you will be.**

> ### Establish Your Mentorship Goal
>
> Before approaching a potential mentor, identify your goal. Define it as well as your intent and purpose. Consider this example:
>
> | Goal Idea | Details | Intention and Purpose |
> |---|---|---|
> | I want to be better at personal branding. | I want to improve my ability to leave a positive impression through my physical presence and confidence. | I will improve my impact on others with a more executive presence. That will increase my confidence around senior leaders, which will help prepare me for my next role at the company. |

A great way to gain clarity on your mentoring desires is to outline a few specific developmental goals with which you would like a mentor to help you. In my experience, you need a significant amount of clarity to write goals well. I've had discussions with thousands of people who would like a mentor; only a fraction of them are willing to sit down and spend time writing detailed goals in advance of initiating the mentoring relationship. Clarity will help you identify the right mentor and help you approach that person with intention and purpose.

Writing developmental goals is a basic practice for talent development professionals, but we are often much better at requiring the practice from others than doing the work ourselves. See the sidebar for a sample draft goal.

Finding a Mentor

Once you know the purpose behind your desire for a mentor, your next step is to tap your resources to find a quality mentor.

Types of Mentoring Relationships

Mentoring relationships typically come in two forms: structured programs and unstructured relationships. Organizations develop structured programs, sometimes called formal mentoring, to increase community and connection across the company. On the other hand, unstructured relationships—also known as organic mentoring relationships—are beyond the confines of a planned program. They may entail learning and growth via social learning within an organization. Or they may be intentional relationships outside of your place of employment, either career-focused or for the purpose of achieving a personal goal or role, such as parenting.

Keep in mind that you don't have to choose between structured and unstructured mentoring if both options are available to you. And if you don't have a formal program available, you can also opt to have multiple mentors for different purposes. You can have various relationships working in tandem to great effect.

Structured Programs

If you are fortunate enough to have access to a structured mentoring program, that's a big leap forward in identifying a mentor. All mentors who are part of the program have expectations with which they will be working with mentees. In many cases, they have enthusiastically signed up to participate in the program and will be open to the idea of your social learning relationship.

Identifying and developing a relationship with a mentor in this scenario is generally easy, because the organization has set out guidelines for how the program will work, job aids and checklists for conversations between the mentor and mentee, and other helpful resources. While the specific program will vary by company—sometimes the mentee asks an individual to be a mentor, sometimes the mentor is chosen for the mentee—each will have guidelines.

Mentors in structured programs are already familiar with the purpose of the mentoring program and the organizational culture, and they are aware of internally available resources that may be useful to mentees. Volunteer mentors are also generally prepared to connect you with other people in their network who can help with your developmental goals.

Beyond these stated benefits, all talent development practitioners who have access to a structured mentoring program should participate. You can gain tremendous benefit from firsthand mentoring experience, connecting with mentors who are senior leaders across the organization, and modeling the same investment in self-development that we ask of talent in our companies.

Unstructured Relationships

Not everyone has access to structured programs. In those cases, we must find and ask a mentor to work with us. It isn't rocket science. But the difference between what you may be doing now and what you should be doing to find a mentor is intention and purpose.

Using an intentional approach to mentoring means having clarity at each step. For example, being intentional about finding a mentor in your field may entail joining local professional events.

Keep in mind that attending events such as a professional organization's chapter meeting or conference is great, but don't wait for an excellent mentor to fall into your lap. Go to the events where potential mentors are going. They likely aren't going to an introduction to instructional design seminar, so you may need to step outside of your comfort zone to find your mentor or recruit others to make introductions. Be creative and proactive.

Further, the process of securing a mentor who will help you achieve your goals doesn't need to be complicated. And while it may seem counterintuitive, select a person who's had failures as well as successes. Oftentimes, it's the mistakes that individuals have made that provide the greatest lessons and opportunities for growth. How a person handles those failures is a great indicator of character and resilience, two important strengths for everyone to cultivate.

Where to Look

For those without a company-offered mentoring program or those who want to expand their mentoring options to include informal relationships, selecting the ideal mentor may feel like a daunting task. One way to alleviate anxiety is to take to heart the idea that you can and should have multiple mentors. As stated previously, there isn't one perfect mentor who can meet all your

Choosing a Mentor

To find a mentor, start by making a list of 20 people. These should be individuals you have more than a passing acquaintance with, because you are going to ask them for a favor. Next to their names, write down one thing they are really good at that you are not but are interested in learning about. For example, one may have an incredible executive presence, while another is a TED speaker, and another is a forward-thinking business owner.

Your initial list may produce the name of a great potential mentor. If so, approach that person with intention and ask for the individual to consider mentoring you in pursuit of your goals.

However, you may not find a strong mentor from this initial list. The next step is to ask the individuals on that list for help. Email or call each individually. Explain your specific vision for success, your goals, and ask whether the person knows of any experts in that specific area. Directly and clearly ask for an introduction. Mentors are more likely to agree to work with you if the introduction is a warm one.

If the list method isn't fruitful, use more conventional ways to find a mentor. Look for people who participate in communities or identify with a specific group. The internet is full of bloggers, authors, and podcasters with amazing legacies and a passion for helping others. Explore online communities of practice and associations where subject matter experts are posting and find someone whose style resonates with you. Attend conferences, trade shows, or local events in the industry and say, "I'm looking for a mentor in X" after you introduce yourself.

needs. Reduce the pressure on yourself and focus on finding a mentor who can help you in one or two areas.

To begin, leverage your network. A job aid at the end of this issue will guide you through an activity to identify individuals in your network and their qualities and characteristics you admire. From there, you can determine which may be able to best help you with your identified purpose.

Obviously, the more colleagues you have in your professional network, the greater the chance you have of finding a great mentor whom you already know. In addition, a large network exponentially increases the chance that, even if you don't have a great person to rely on as a mentor in your immediate network, your colleagues may know someone who could be a good fit. For example, you can use LinkedIn to ask your first-level connections to introduce you to someone with whom they're connected.

Approaching a Mentor

For some, inviting an individual to be their mentor is as stressful as public speaking or asking someone out for a first date. There is something scary about asking a person to be heavily involved in your career trajectory. By asking

Requesting a Mentor

The way in which you approach and ask an individual to be your mentor can affect their likelihood to commit. Put yourself in a potential mentor's shoes. Imagine you receive two emails from individuals in the marketing department. You don't know either of them.

Dear Bev,

I have heard a lot about you, and my boss told me you would make a good mentor. Would you mentor me? Let me know what you think.

Thank you!

Laila

Dear Bev,

You were recommended to me by Declan in the HR department as someone who has done extensive work in compensation bracketing and classification. That's one of my developmental areas this year. I was wondering if you would be willing to meet with me to share your experience. If we both find the meeting valuable, I'm hoping you will consider mentoring me in this area for six months.

Please let me know what questions you may have. I'm looking forward to the conversation!

Thank you,

Rowan

Based on their requests, consider which of the two individuals you are most likely to say yes to. Now consider why.

Rowan's message is longer and more detailed, but why does that matter? Rowan's message demonstrates that he is more prepared, more proactive, and clearer on what he wants from a mentoring relationship. He is specific in terms of what he is asking for as well as the length of time; he has provided a specific rationale for why he is asking you; and he gives you an opportunity to meet but opt out of mentoring if the meeting is not valuable. In this way, Rowan is managing expectations.

that person to be your mentor, you are being vulnerable, especially because your proposed mentor is someone whom you respect for their knowledge, presence, or other attribute.

While you're feeling vulnerable, it's likely that the person whom you approach will feel flattered that you have asked. How you ask the person will vary. Are you reaching out to a connection on LinkedIn? Is this someone whom you have heard speak at a conference and whom you admire for the subject matter about which the individual spoke? If so, you're likely to message that person electronically.

Do you want to approach someone with whom you've had a working or professional relationship? Perhaps a local chapter of an association has an email directory for everyone in the chapter. Or you may want to establish an informal mentoring relationship with someone whom you feel does a great job at keeping her personal and professional life in order—managing to volunteer, being active in her children's activities, and furthering her career, among other aspects. If you interact with this individual, determine whether a face-to-face conversation or email is best for asking the individual to serve as your mentor.

If the person declines to be your mentor, they will likely either say no and explain why or will suggest someone who could be your mentor. Most people won't say no because they think you are a terrible professional and not worth their time. Generally, it's because they have—or feel they have—constraints that will get in the way of them being a good mentor.

Some people who choose not to mentor feel that their current workload or personal duties will create distractions or a time crunch that will take their attention away from their work with you. Others wrestle with some version of imposter syndrome, feeling they don't have much to offer or don't have the skills necessary to be a good mentor. So, if someone politely refuses your request, remember it's not a personal rejection.

In my experience, most people jump at the opportunity to mentor others. After all, people naturally appreciate that someone else sees value in who they are and what they have to offer. Most are willing to mentor others as long as they can justify the effort and time commitment. The more you can make the mentor role feel easy for the individual, the more likely the individual is to say yes. See the Requesting a Mentor sidebar for further considerations to keep in mind.

> **If someone politely refuses your request, remember it's not a personal rejection.**

Once your prospective mentor has agreed to the relationship, it's time to set up a meeting to discuss what you hope to gain from the relationship and how you believe that person can help. Whether the individual is in your community, across the country, or on another continent will be an important factor in whether you arrange to meet in person, via Skype or FaceTime, or via phone. And, of course, if this is part of a structured mentoring program within your organization, it's likely you'll meet at the office or perhaps at a nearby coffee shop.

During the meeting, be sure to demonstrate your genuine enthusiasm for your work and that you are taking an active interest in your future. After all, the prospective mentor will be making the effort and time commitment to serve as your mentor.

You also need to show that you are open to feedback, even for things that may be hard for you to hear, as well as that you are committed to learning. Those are essential building blocks to getting the relationship off to a strong start and creating trust with your mentor.

In addition to the enthusiasm and showing that you're open to feedback, some of the matters you'll want to discuss are how you'll meet, the frequency of those meetings, what success will look like, how long you expect to continue the relationship, and how to end the relationship if one of you feels it is necessary to do so because of lack of success.

The Mentorship

Working with a mentor is an ongoing and, hopefully lasting, process. In the talent development industry, we put a lot of emphasis on the first couple of steps—looking for a mentor, asking the individual to be your mentor, and having your first conversation. However, the majority of your time will be spent for months, and maybe years, working together toward your agreed-upon goals. As such, it is important to take time to structure and develop a strong relationship, as well as set goals (as I will discuss later in this issue).

Structuring the Relationship

How you structure your mentorship will likely change over time, but in general, I've found that you should meet more frequently at the beginning. From there, the relationship will naturally begin to evolve. I recommend meeting every two weeks for a couple of months to establish the foundational elements; then move to once a month for a year. Monthly meetings tend to have enough time in between so that you can apply what you are working on but not so long that you lose accountability.

Plan for regular check-ins with your mentor regarding the relationship. Every few conversations should include some time for discussing these questions:
- Are we meeting frequently enough or too frequently to be valuable?
- Do we have enough time scheduled, or do we keep cutting conversations short?
- Is the format of our meeting (face-to-face, video meeting platform, or other means) contributing to the success of this relationship, or should we use a different method?
- Are we satisfied with the process of setting and confirming meetings?
- What should we change about the structure, flow, or agenda of our meetings?

Throughout a mentoring relationship, your comfort level should grow. Over time, you should start to feel more at ease with being authentic and more relaxed talking about your wins and misses. Be aware of your balance of professional authenticity. You should cultivate a deep level of trust and share things about yourself within reason.

The greater level of comfort should also enable you and your mentor to have more open conversations about feedback. If your mentor does not freely provide both positive and critical feedback, be sure to ask for it. Growth in a mentoring relationship evolves, in part, from hearing observations and feedback from a mentor you trust.

Developing a Strong Relationship

There are several key elements to a strong relationship between mentor and mentee, just as there are with other relationships, both personal and professional.

Professional Authenticity

One of the most important principles of truly effective mentoring is the idea of showing up. As a mentee, you should be comfortable sharing your true, authentic self. You should build your mentoring relationships on honesty and open communication. Your authenticity will encourage your mentor (or mentors) to likewise be authentic, leading to trust and respect.

Be aware that showing up as your authentic self doesn't necessarily mean you should share everything. You can be yourself without delving into topics of conversation that will make your mentor uncomfortable. This balance is called *professional authenticity*. At the beginning of a mentoring relationship, it's always a good idea to discuss frankly with your mentor those topics that each of you feels should remain outside the parameters of your relationship.

Mutual Trust and Respect

Mentoring only works if it's rooted in deep mutual trust and respect. You can't achieve them if you're unable to authentically be yourself. If your mentor is daunting to you or you're worried the individual is somehow more important, famous, or successful than you, you must either voice that and unpack it together or find a new mentor. You won't be able to fully challenge yourself and lean forward if you're too worried about what to say or wear or whether you are good enough for your mentor.

Intentionally build mutual trust and respect. You know you are a trustworthy person; your new mentor likely is as well. However, that doesn't mean you both will automatically be great at building trust in the

> **Mentoring only works if it's rooted in deep mutual trust and respect.**

relationship. Because mentoring is a different kind of relationship dynamic, landing in both professional and personal areas, it's important that you communicate with your mentor about trust. Do so through actions as well as mannerisms and body language. Maintain confidences, show respect, and be honest—those are all aspects of establishing trust within a relationship. To continue to build trust, make sure you are vigilant about setting and keeping meetings, taking notes, and following up on commitments.

Expectations and Boundaries

Unsurprising, setting expectations and boundaries is important to a successful mentoring relationship. Some new mentoring partners don't set explicit boundaries, or they fail to discuss expectations for their roles. After all, it may seem awkward to start a new relationship by talking about ground rules on what topics are out of bounds or who will set up new meetings. However, as challenging as it may seem to broach that conversation, it's far more difficult to overcome an issue later.

I remember one mentor sharing an experience she had that resulted from a lack of expectations. She had started working with a mentee on some professional goals, and it was going well. A few months into the relationship, the mentee started arriving late to meetings and sometimes didn't do the work he had committed to in previous meetings. The mentor was exasperated and felt disrespected. She wanted to part ways, but when she talked to the mentee, he had no idea of the impact of his behavior. He didn't know that he was not meeting her expectations, because they had never set any, and he lost his mentor because of it.

One handy tool for discussing authenticity, trust, boundaries, and expectations with your mentor is a mentoring agreement. It is a checklist that helps you and your mentor ensure your relationship starts on the right path. Mentoring agreements have fallen out of favor recently, but that's mostly because people have used them poorly in the past and the agreements have gained a bad reputation because of it. Individuals would disregard the agreement or fail to follow through on the tenets they agreed to—such as adhering to the schedule and showing up on time.

Using a mentoring agreement in the right way means leveraging it as a framework for your first conversation and then following through on the agreement. By doing so, you demonstrate respect. A sample mentoring agreement job aid is included at the end of this issue.

Focus on the Journey

It's cliché but true: Mentoring is a journey, not a destination. We tend to think that mentoring happens when you sit down with an expert and absorb the individual's wisdom. However, the reality is that we learn between those meetings. Your mentor may share incredible insights and trigger aha moments, but your development begins when you apply those ideas in your job and life. As you take a nugget of advice or think about the great question that your mentor asked and look at how it fits into your work, you are growing.

Think about it this way: Imagine you have an idea for a completely life-changing invention. It's unique and useful, and the market for it is tremendous. However, you never develop or even prototype it. The idea just sits in your head and becomes a failed idea because no one ever saw it. The same is true for what's discussed in a mentoring relationship. I've had mentors share some insightful and powerful ideas with me, but if I don't take those ideas and apply them and make them my own, I don't develop.

Making Developmental Goals

You cannot just arrive at your scheduled mentoring meeting time, have a great conversation, go home, repeat monthly, and expect to learn. Conversely, if you treat the mentoring conversations as catalysts for the work you commit to between meetings, that's a recipe for success.

Because the focus is on the journey, I have created a mentoring road map that you can use to identify where you are starting and the path to your destination—that is, your developmental goals. Use a different road map for each goal. Break the goal down into smaller, manageable action steps. Your mentor will help with that, based on their level of expertise in that skill or attribute.

The map provides a basic structure for you to identify key checkpoints along the way during your mentoring relationship. Checkpoints are activities, tasks, and deliverables that will help you make progress on your goals. They serve as a method for assessing your progress throughout the relationship.

Consider the personal branding sample goal from the Establish Your Mentorship Goal sidebar. To achieve this goal, the mentee may use checkpoints such as:
- observing three colleagues with strong executive presence
- participating in a public speaking course
- role-playing stressful situations
- reading two books about confidence or imposter syndrome
- starting a peer mentoring group on the topic.

Take Time to Give Back

Another piece of the journey that will be beneficial to you is to think about how you can reciprocate your mentor's investment. As you develop your relationship, you will get to know more about your mentor's role in their organization. Finding ways to give back in the relationship enables you to make the relationship mutually beneficial. Certainly, if you are in a structured mentoring relationship, let the program manager know how your mentor is helping you. And in the increasingly social media world, you can give back via professional networks. Some ways to do that are:
- introducing your mentor to your network
- giving perspectives from your demographic, if it applies to a project your mentor is working on
- sharing new frameworks, technologies, and methods that your mentor may be unfamiliar with
- showing your mentor how to use new technologies
- letting others know of your mentor's strengths
- offering to help on projects in ways that you can.

The best mentoring relationships will provide benefits to both you and your mentor in different ways.

> **Finding ways to give back in the relationship enables you to make the relationship mutually beneficial.**

Detours

Not all journeys follow a straight path. Some require detours, and the mentorship journey can be the same. Even the best-laid mentoring plans will occasionally get upturned by real-life obstacles. Although you and your mentor may have done a fantastic job of identifying goals, building trust, and mapping out your plan, remain flexible. Small detours from your road map could include a more pressing topic that takes up a few meetings and delays other planned work. Larger detours occur when something happens that takes you or your mentor away from the mentoring relationship for a period of time.

In any case, it's important that you address the detours openly and discuss how you both want to navigate them. Remember, however, that these are simply detours and do not need to be roadblocks to the mentoring relationship. In fact, in the end, they can make the mentoring relationship stronger and more valuable.

Wrapping Up the Relationship

All formal relationships must eventually come to an end. If you are participating in a mentoring program, your relationship may have a scheduled end date corresponding to the program cycle. If you are in a relationship outside of a formal program, you can use check-in points and goal attainment to determine what signals a natural point to conclude the mentorship. You may choose to continue to meet informally with your mentor or transition the formal relationship into a different kind of relationship moving forward.

Take Time to Reflect

For your last formal mentoring conversation, reflect with your mentor on the process, goals, and transition. Use this list of questions to get the conversation started.

Process
- Were the processes you and your mentor put into place successful in terms of duration and communications?
- Did both of you consistently attend the agreed-upon meetings?
- Were meeting times convenient for both?
- Were the meetings of the appropriate length for desired conversations?

Communication
- Apart from meetings, did you and your mentor feel that the frequency of communication was adequate?
- Was the communication format (such as email, phone, or social media) of liking to each of you?
- Did you give back to your mentor?
- How did you overcome obstacles or roadblocks that occurred during the mentoring relationship?

Goals
- Did you accomplish your goals, or were you happy with the progress you made on your initial goals?
- Was the progress toward goals made at a rate that suited both parties?
- Did you and your mentor agree to checkpoints early in the relationship and discuss those as appropriate?
- Did you openly and honestly discuss obstacles?
- Does your mentor have any additional feedback for you?
- What new goals do you have?

Transition
- Do either of you have any comments that you have not already discussed?
- Have you taken time to acknowledge and celebrate the accomplishments and relationship?
- Are you considering new goals?
- Does the mentor have learning opportunities to share with you?
- What are your and your mentor's expectations moving forward—such as staying in touch or severing the relationship?

People often overlook the ending of a mentorship. Some mentoring partners just drift away from each other, meeting less and less frequently. Sometimes they stop meeting all together. But this is a missed opportunity. You've worked so hard throughout the mentoring relationship—be sure to have a final meeting to celebrate and review.

In all cases, acknowledge the work you've done and the progress you and your mentor have made. Both of you should reflect on your growth during the relationship and revisit the developmental goals. Spend time examining the relationship to learn from the experience. Discuss what aspects of the logistics, tools, communication methods and preferences, assignments, and milestones worked well for each of you. Clearly identify areas of the relationship that you each could improve on for future mentoring relationships.

Finally, celebrate the success of your relationship—you've worked hard, and the work you both have done deserves celebrating. You each have invested time, energy, and effort. The last conversation is a perfect time to recognize what you've accomplished together and show gratitude to each other. Regardless of whether you plan to transition to a different type of relationship (such as a more social one) or simply part ways, mutually agree on a time to celebrate, whether that is going out for a meal together or even a virtual coffee chat, if you aren't geographically close, or getting each other a small token gift to commemorate the mentoring relationship. Work with your mentor to decide what is appropriate and valuable to both of you.

Conclusion

As a talent development practitioner, you may have unique insights into learning and mentoring. However, that doesn't mean you personally have the experience of working with an effective mentor. I have encountered numerous practitioners who take care of everyone else's L&D before their own. Numerous of individuals I have worked with personally are tasked with building mentoring programs for their organizations but have never had a mentor before. Regardless of whether you are new to the field or are a seasoned veteran, mentoring is essential for professional growth and development.

Now is your chance. Use the ideas in this issue of *TD at Work* to identify your own skills gaps. Using the exercise described earlier in this issue, identify one or more mentors with whom you'd like to work. Approach them with clarity, intention, and purpose. At the start of your mentoring relationship, set goals, build trust, and establish expectations and boundaries. Work with your mentor using the mentoring agreement and road maps provided in this issue. And when you have accomplished your goals or when things have changed and it's time to move on, be purposeful about concluding your mentoring relationship.

Finally, be sure to reciprocate. After you've had a truly valuable mentoring experience, find someone who needs a mentor and extend yourself to that individual.

References & Resources

Books

Campbell, J., and P. Cousineau (ed.). 2014. *The Hero's Journey: Joseph Campbell on His Life and Work (The Collected Works of Joseph Campbell)*. 3rd ed. Novato, California: New World Library.

Labin, J. 2017. *Mentoring Programs That Work*. Alexandria, VA: ATD Press.

Research Report

ATD Research. 2017. *Mentoring Matters: Developing Talent With Formal Mentoring Programs*. Alexandria, VA: ATD Press.

Online Resources

Association for Talent Development. n.d. "What Is Mentoring?" www.td.org/what-is-mentoring.

Emrich, C., M.H. Livingston, D. Pruner, L. Oberfeld, and S. Page. 2017. *Creating a Culture of Mentorship*. Heidrick & Struggles, December 27. www.heidrick.com/Knowledge-Center/Publication/Creating_a_culture_of_mentorship.

Labin, J. 2019. "If Someone Asks You to Be Their Mentor, Say 'Yes.'" Recruiter.com, April 22. www.recruiter.com/i/if-someone-asks-you-to-be-their-mentor-say-yes.

Lombardozzi, C. 2018. "How Can Talent Development Professionals Support Social Learning in the Workplace?" Learning 4 Learning Professionals, March 20. https://l4lp.com/curated-resources/social-learning.

MacCartney, P. 2019. "Using Mentoring Technology to Measure and Maximize ROI." International Mentoring School, Nov. 6. www.internationalmentoringschool.com/blogmentoring/mentoring-technology-measure-maximize-roi.

Panopto. 2019. "What Is Social Learning, and Why Is It So Important for Corporate Learning & Development?" Jan. 16. www.panopto.com/blog/what-is-social-learning-and-why-is-it-so-important-for-corporate-ld.

Sancier-Sultan, S., and J. Sperling-Magro. 2019. "Taking the lead for inclusion." McKinsey, November. www.mckinsey.com/featured-insights/gender-equality/taking-the-lead-for-inclusion.

Job Aid

Mentoring Agreement Template

Review this example mentoring agreement and then use the template to outline specifics of your mentoring relationship, including frequency and type of meetings, goals, and ground rules.

Example

Date: February 21, 2020	
Mentee: Kim David	
Mentor: Juan Rodriguez	
Expectations/Conduct	
Mentee: I am asking my mentor to help me with my management skills. This will entail suggesting podcasts and TED Talks, online print resources, and role-play scenarios. I will journal to reflect on what I have learned and will ask my mentor to offer feedback on my progress. I respect and appreciate the time and guidance my mentor is giving me.	**Additional Comments:**
Mentor: I expect my mentee to be fully committed to progressing in her management development. I commit to acting in the best interest of my mentee with diplomacy and patience. I will not make decisions for my mentee; rather, I will ask questions for my mentee to consider and offer feedback on her progression. I will share my knowledge and expertise with my mentee.	**Additional Comments:**
Confidentiality	We will treat all communications as confidential unless we agree otherwise or they fall under certain confidentiality exceptions (e.g., we believe harm may come to the person or others).
Communication and Meetings	We will strive to meet every week for the first month and once every month thereafter for 12 months, at which time we will revisit the issue.
	Additionally, we will connect via phone, email, or a virtual meeting every Friday.
Closing the Relationship	Either of us may terminate the relationship at any time. We will agree to discuss our decision with one another, in a no-fault manner.
Mentee Signature:	
Mentor Signature:	

Job Aid

Mentoring Agreement Template (Cont.)

Template

Date:	
Mentee:	
Mentor:	
Expectations/Conduct	
Mentee:	Additional Comments:
Mentor:	Additional Comments:
Confidentiality	
Communication and Meetings	
Closing the Relationship	
Mentee Signature:	
Mentor Signature:	

Job Aid

Mentorship Road Map

Chart your story using prompts and milestones. When mapping out your story, identify where you are and how you ended up there.

- Who helped you along the way?
- What advice or feedback did you receive?
- What mistakes did you make?
- How did your strengths and passions serve you?
- What books, videos, training, conferences, or events helped you?
- Was your path winding or straightforward?